BOOGIE WOOGIE HANON

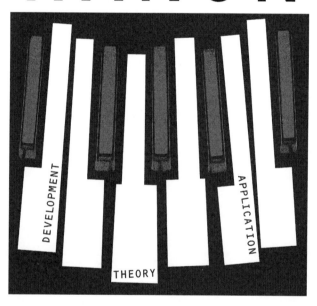

Published by

HAL LEONARD

Exclusive Distributors:

HAL LEONARD
7777 West Bluemound Road
Milwaukee, WI 53213
Email: info@halleonard.com

HAL LEONARD EUROPE LIMITED
42 Wigmore Street
Marylebone, London, W1U 2RN
Email: info@halleonardeurope.com

HAL LEONARD AUSTRALIA PTY. LTD.
4 Lentara Court
Cheltenham, Victoria, 3192 Australia
Email: info@halleonard.com.au

Order No. AM1004630

ISBN 978-1-78038-523-5

Written by Leo Alfassy.

Edited by Brenda Murphy.

Introduction by Graham Vickers.

Cover designed by Michael Bell Design.

BOOGIE WOOGIE HANON

CONTENTS

The origins of the boogie-woogie piano style lie in what happened to the blues when the agricultural American South started to become industrialized. Poor African-American communities could no longer depend upon traditional work on the land and so the first Great Migration began. It saw the relocation of some two million black workers to the cities of the North, the Midwest and the West.

Those who gravitated towards the lumber camps of Texas seem to have joined the vanguard of the inchoate boogie-woogie, a style which some sources identify as having started as early as the 1870s in the Piney Woods territory of north-east Texas. Even so, it was that mass migration in the early part of the 20th century that established this up-tempo piano-based style as *the* hot music for dancing in the urban music dives of the Northern and Midwest slums.

The boogie-woogie is a heavily percussive piano style, characterized by short melodic phrases of great rhythmic variety (riffs) played against a constantly reiterated (ostinato) bass pattern with hands usually far apart. The style attracted many pianists who might play for staggeringly long hours at rent house parties as well as the in the barrel houses (primitive bars where the storage barrels formed the seating) that lent their name to a particularly wild improvised offshoot of the boogie-woogie piano style.

Boogie-woogie itself was essentially a self-taught style based on improvisation. Determining factors included a rough and noisy audience and instruments that were unlikely to be in prime condition; this was no milieu for subtlety and tonal modulation. What it demanded and got was a percussive approach based on simple single-note melodic phrases and a repetitious rhythmic bass pattern. Developed from the blues, the boogie-woogie had to abandon both the inspiration and the spare technique of its origins.

The southern blues had been a voice-led, non-commercial, slow-tempo expression of quiet despair performed at a medium dynamic level. Boogie was a fast-tempo instrumental style played at a high dynamic level, often as part of a rudimentary dance band and usually for payment, however modest.

Following its hazy birth in north-east Texas boogie-woogie sprang up in Kansas City, Memphis, St.Louis, and perhaps most significantly, in Chicago. Chicago was where a new generation of pianists, some of whom had received a musical education, developed a richer harmonic and stylistic vocabulary. Gentrified, the style began to be heard in more respectable establishments and eventually made it to the recording studios and a wider audience.

In the 1920s and 1930s the great popularizer of boogie-woogie was Meade 'Lux' Lewis. Along with Pete Johnson and Albert Ammons (both of whom appeared in a famous show with Lewis at Manhattan's Carnegie Hall in 1938), Lewis brought boogie-woogie a degree of respectability.

The second half of the 1940s saw the development of a more sophisticated boogie-woogie style, especially after the introduction of electrically amplified instruments in the bands that performed it. By the 1950s, however, the style was going into decline as rock'n'roll began to emerge, although country music had adopted and adapted it in the 1940s to create country boogie where the instrumentation might vary but the broad rhythmic style was retained.

Country pianist Moon Mullican was closely associated with a hillbilly boogie style, brother duet The Delmore Brothers had a hit with 'Freight Train Boogie' and even the more mainstream Tennessee Ernie Ford recorded several boogies including his No.1 hit 'The Shotgun Boogie.'

The 'boogie' tag persists into contemporary music and intermittent revivals of the real thing come and go. If its golden age is long gone, what remains is the vitality and excitement of boogie-woogie's hypnotic, repeated rhythmic patterns and its use of the piano to parlay the haunting hard-times vocal tradition of the blues into vibrant good-time music.

Graham Vickers

The music in this book is divided into two parts. The exercises in
the first part are devoted primarily to the development of the agility
and evenness of the finger action of the left hand. The basic boogie
patterns are presented in C major and in order of increasing difficulty,
from the simplest quarter-note figure to the most elaborate dotted
eighth-note bass line.

The second part covers the most important melodic patterns of the
boogie as performed by the greatest pianists in the field. This idiomatic
melodic language is super-imposed upon the familiar bass patterns
from the first part, but transposed into the most frequently-used keys.
Also in this section are the exercises needed for the absolute
independence, and at the same time coordination, of both hands.

Because the playing of boogie-woogie requires an extraordinary
independence of hands, it is absolutely necessary to practice each
hand separately. It is also strongly advised not to use the right pedal,
which would destroy the intrinsic worth of this particular piano style.
Instead, the student can keep a steady tempo by tapping the beat
with the right foot.

The first few sections explain the characteristic features of the boogie
in relation to the basic elements of music. They also contain examples
of typical introductions and endings, as well as performance practices.

Elements of Boogie Style

Melody

The melodic line of the boogie cannot be described, in a strict sense, as a succession of single tones perceived by the mind as a unity. The characteristic boogie melody consists either of a short motive reiterated in innumerable rhythmic variations, or of a succession of disparate motivic fragments combined in a twelve-bar formal structure. A motive can consist of only one or two notes constantly repeated (a), or it can be a short musical phrase (b).

Very often several initial eighth notes precede the melody in form of an upbeat.

In order to follow the changing harmony, musical phrases can be altered chromatically (a), or transposed to another pitch above or below (b).

The melodic line often contains melodic features typical of the blues, namely the so-called "blue" notes. These are notes, particularly the third and seventh degrees of the scale, whose intonation lies *between* the major and the minor pitches. In blues singing, these notes could be easily performed by the singer or played on the guitar, the most important instrument for blues accompaniment. In order to imitate the blue notes which were impossible to play on a keyboard instrument, the boogie pianists had to develop a special technique of embellishments consisting of grace notes and slides.

Grace Notes, Slides, and Tremolos

In classical music, the time value of a grace note (note printed in small type) must be subtracted from that of the preceding or following notes. In the interpretation of boogie, the value of the grace note is extremely short—in other words, the grace note and the adjacent note are played almost simultaneously *on* the beat. This extremely short value is achieved through the sliding of the same finger from a black to a white key on the keyboard.

Because it is impossible to slide with the same finger from one white to another white key, or from a white to a black key, two fingers are necessary to perform the grace note and the adjacent note.

To create an even greater illusion of guitar playing, the blues pianist often strikes simultaneously two notes situated a semitone apart (a). The agglomeration of a few semitones in the same chord, called "tone cluster," adds more excitement to the inherent drive of the boogie (b).

The tremolo is a device frequently used in boogie. It occurs in the form of quickly repeated notes, mostly thirds and octaves.

Sometimes the tremolo consists of whole chords, performed with one or both hands (a). Very often it is preceded by grace notes or slurs (b).

Harmony and Form

The harmonic and formal structures of the boogie are the same as the blues. Every composition consists of a succession of twelve-bar sections called "choruses," each section containing an identical harmonic pattern. This pattern is based on the triads built over the first (tonic), fourth (subdominant), and fifth (dominant) degrees of the scale. Here is the formal and harmonic structure of a typical blues or boogie in the key of C.

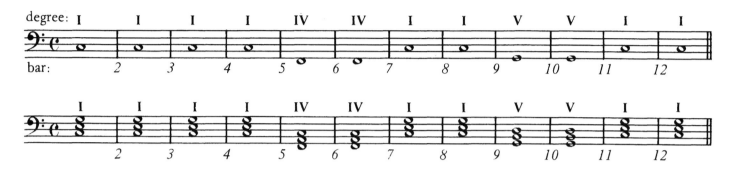

Sometimes the tonic triads of measures 2 and 10 are replaced by the subdominant triad or a dominant seventh chord.

There are many exceptions to this basic harmonic pattern. The great performers of blues and boogie use sophisticated chords, tone clusters, and strikingly original harmonic progressions within this fundamental framework.

Here is a modern version of the blues (or boogie) form. Note the characteristic chord progression in the last two measures.

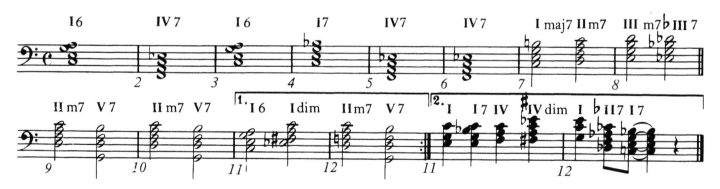

Bass Line

The most characteristic feature of boogie is its bass line, which has to play a double role: as a harmonic support, and as a replacement for the rhythm section of a band. With the exception of a few "breaks," the rhythmic pulse of the left hand is always there and has to be kept steady from beginning to end. A simple bass figure can consist of only four quarter notes per bar, or the repetition of open fifths or chords.

The bass line can also consist of the so-called "walking bass" (notes "walking" up and down the scale or in broken chords), probably derived from the common bass patterns of jazz bassists.

But usually the bass figure contains eight eighth notes to the bar, which is what gave boogie the name "Eight to the Bar." There are innumerable examples of bass figures; the most common of them are covered in the special exercises for the left hand.

Meter and Rhythm

The meter of the boogie is, with rare exceptions, **C** (common) or **¢** (*alla breve*).

The rhythm in the early boogie was relatively simple: the bass figures were mostly without dotted notes, the right hand repeating short riffs over and over again. Gradually the style became more and more sophisticated, revealing sometimes an incredible polyrhythmic complexity. In some performances by famous pianists one can find three, five, or seven notes in the treble against eight notes in the bass—a rhythmic excitement rarely found in other styles.

Jazz music contains multiple layers of rhythmic activity occuring simultaneously at different rates of pulse in the main musical elements—melody, harmony, and rhythm. By contrast, what makes the boogie particularly exciting is the fact that the melody (consisting often of eighth and sixteenth notes) is superimposed upon an accompaniment which also moves fast in short time values. The harmonic progressions take place at a much slower pace—a single chord often stretched over four bars—thus creating a rhythmic counterpoint to the other faster-moving elements.

The following diagrams illustrate three typical examples of rhythmic superimposition found in the boogie-woogie.

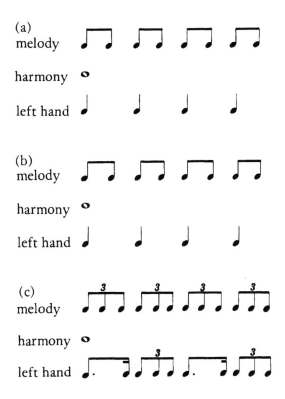

Introductions and Endings

Very characteristic of the boogie is the fact that the introduction is not a special fragment preceding the chorus, but is played *instead* of the first four bars, followed by the usual eight remaining bars of the twelve-bar structure.

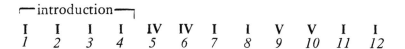

The introduction can consist of tremolos in both hands without a beat (a), whole-tone chords or "breaks" in the left hand (b), or a modulating passage finishing on IV (subdominant) in the fifth bar (c).

Contrary to the rules of traditional harmony, the piece can finish on a dominant seventh or other seventh chords.

Exercises—Part I

1.

2.

3.

11.

rall.

12.

14.

15.

16.

17.

18.

19.

20.

21.

22.

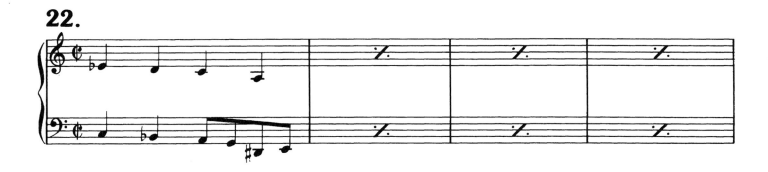

23.

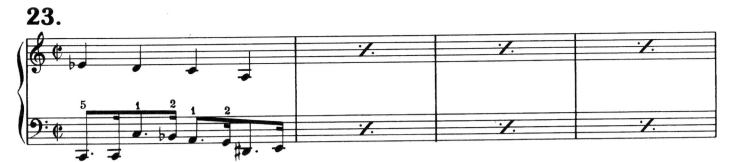

24.

27.

28.

29.

30.

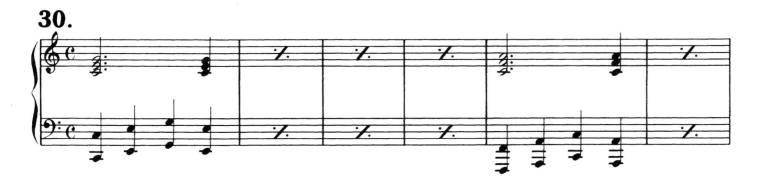

31.

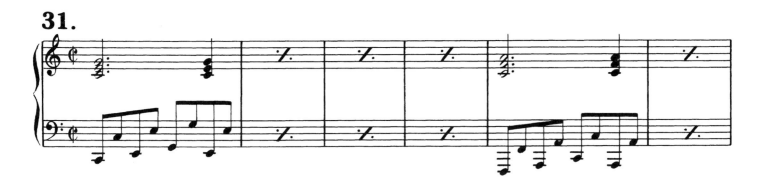

35.

36.

37.

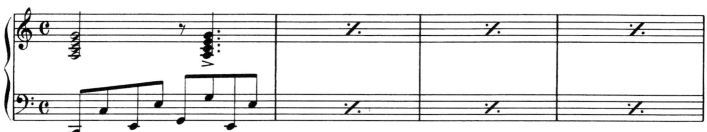

38.

41.

42.

43.

44.

45.

46.

47.

48.

51.

52.

53.

54.

55.

56.

57.

58.

59.

60.

61.

62.

63.

64.

65.

66.

67.

68.

69.

70.

71.

72.

Exercises—Part II

75.

76.

80.

rhythmic independence of hands

81.

82.

84.

85.

87.

88.

89.

91.

95.

96.

100.